Heather —

Happy Mother's Day
2007. I hope as you
enjoy this book you will
reflect on the important work
you are doing, that Mother's child
is a bond that will never
break. I love you.

Mom

ERRAND *of* ANGELS

In Honor and Praise of Mothers

Cover image *Something to Treasure* © 2007 Jean Monti, licensed by The Greenwich Workshop, Inc. www.greenwichworkshop.com.
Cover and book design by Jessica A. Warner, © 2007 by Covenant Communications, Inc.
Published by Covenant Communications, Inc., American Fork, Utah

Printed in Canada
First Printing: March 2007

13 12 11 10 09 08 07   10 9 8 7 6 5 4 3 2 1

ISBN 978-1-59811-341-9

ERRAND *of* ANGELS

In Honor and Praise of Mothers

Make a memory with your children,

Spend some time to show you care;

Toys and trinkets can't replace those

Precious moments that you share.

ELAINE HARDT

A MOTHER

When God set the world in place,
When He hung the stars up in space,
When He made the land and the sea -
Then, He made you and me.

He sat back and saw all that was good.
He saw things to be as they should.
Just one more blessing He had in store.
He created a mother. But, whatever for?

He knew a mother would have a special place
To shine His reflection on her child's face.
A mother will walk the extra mile,
Just to see her children smile.

She'll work her fingers to the bone
To make a house into a home.
A mother is there to teach and guide.
A mother will stay right by your side.

She'll be there through your pain and strife.
She'll stay constant in your life.
A mother will lend a helping hand
Until you have the strength to stand.

She'll pick you up when you are down.
When you need a friend, she'll stick around.
A mother is one who listens well,
Will keep her word; will never tell.

A mother never pokes or pries,
But stands, quietly, by your side;
Giving you the strength you need,
Encouraging you to succeed.

A mother is one who can be strong
When you need someone to lean on.
You're more than a mother to me;
A reflection of God, in your face, I see . . .

A love that knows no boundaries.
I'm glad that you chose to be
All this, and more, to me.

You share a love that knows no end.
You're more than my mother.
You are my friend.

KARI KESHMIRY

The mother loves her child most divinely, not when she surrounds him with comfort and anticipates his wants, but when she resolutely holds him to the highest standards and is content with nothing less than his best.

HAMILTON WRIGHT MABIE

omen are the
real architects of society.

HARRIET BEECHER STOWE

The love a grandmother shares
with her little ones, it is a love
that binds the past and the future.

ANONYMOUS

Mothers hold their children's
hands for a little while
and their hearts forever.

———————

The heart of a mother

is a deep abyss

at the bottom of which

you will always find forgiveness.

The true worth of a race

must be measured by

the character of its womanhood.

MARY MCLEOD BETHUNE

The sweetest sounds to mortals given
Are heard in Mother, Home, and Heaven.

WILLIAM GOLDSMITH BROWN

No matter what you read or hear, no matter what the differences of circumstances you observe in the lives of women about you, it is important for you Latter-day Saint women to understand that the Lord holds motherhood and mothers sacred and in the highest esteem. He has entrusted to his daughters the great responsibility of bearing and nurturing children. . . . There is divinity in each new life.

SPENCER W. KIMBALL

Rock Me to Sleep

Mother, dear mother, the years have been long

Since I last listened your lullaby song:

Sing, then, and unto my soul it shall seem

Womanhood's years have been only a dream.

Clasped to your heart in a loving embrace,

With your light lashes just sweeping my face,

Never hereafter to wake or to weep;—

Rock me to sleep, mother,—rock me to sleep!

Elizabeth (Akers) Allen

When the real history of mankind is fully disclosed, will it feature the echoes of gunfire or the shaping sound of lullabies? The great armistices made by military men or the peacemaking of women in homes and in neighborhoods? Will what happened in cradles and kitchens prove to be more controlling than what happened in congresses? When the surf of the centuries has made the great pyramids so much sand, the everlasting family will still be standing, because it is a celestial institution, formed outside telestial time. The women of God know this.

NEAL A. MAXWELL

The real religion of the world
comes from women
much more than from men—
from mothers most of all,
who carry the key of our souls
in their bosoms.

OLIVER WENDELL HOLMES SR.

As we age, we begin to realize
the value of a mother's love
and the enormous depth
of her commitment to us.
No other relationship we form
can ever be as close or profound
as that with our mothers.

ANONYMOUS

THE HAND THAT ROCKS THE CRADLE

Blessing on the hand of women!
Angels guard its strength and grace,
In the palace, cottage, hovel,
Oh, no matter where the place;
Would that never storms assailed it,
Rainbows ever gently curled;
For the hand that rocks the cradle
Is the hand that rules the world. . . .

Blessings on the hand of women!
Fathers, sons, and daughters cry,
And the sacred song is mingled
With the worship in the sky—
Mingles where no tempest darkens,
Rainbows evermore are hurled;
For the hand that rocks the cradle
Is the hand that rules the world.

WILLIAM ROSS WALLACE

other is the one we count on for all the things that matter most of all.

Katharine Butler Hathaway

MY LEGACY

One day I said to the Lord,

"Lord, can you make me immortal?

Is there a way I could live on here forever?"

And the Lord gave me children and grandchildren

and now, I live on through the eyes and smiles,

the hearts and the journeys

of my precious babes and their babies.

LUSIANA AUSTIN

A WONDERFUL MOTHER

God made a wonderful mother,

A mother who never grows old;

He made her smile of the sunshine,

And He molded her heart of pure gold;

In her eyes He placed bright shining stars,

In her cheeks, fair roses you see;

God made a wonderful mother,

And He gave that dear mother to me.

PAT O'REILLY

My mother was the most beautiful woman I ever saw. All I am I owe to my mother. I attribute all my success in life to the moral, intellectual and physical education I received from her.

GEORGE WASHINGTON

As I come to understand the many talents and characteristics of women, I realize how needed their strengths are in this dispensation. We must remember that we are daughters of God here to provide nurturing care for one another, family and friends— loving care to soften the changes of life felt by all.

What a great opportunity we have to fill our God-given role. He has given us the privilege to shape the lives of those entrusted to our care. Even those of us who have not been blessed to have children of our own can still be influential as trainers and nurturers. It does not matter where we live, whether we are rich or poor, whether our family is large or small. Each of us can share that Christ-like love in our "motherly ministry."

Barbara W. Winder

There are times when only a Mother's faith

Can help us on life's way

And inspire in us the confidence

We need from day to day.

For a Mother's heart and a Mother's faith

And a Mother's steadfast love

Were fashioned by the Angels

And sent from God above.

ANONYMOUS

It is not what you do *for* your children, but what you have taught them to *do for themselves* that will make them successful human beings.

Ann Landers

Beyond all lessons, beyond the model she provided, my mother gave me a parent's ultimate gift: she made me feel lovable and good. She paid attention; she listened; she remembered what I said. She did not think me perfect, but she accepted me, without qualification.

FREDELLE MAYNARD

MOTHER—

that was the bank

where we deposited

all our hurts and worries.

T. DeWitt Talmage

I love my mother for all the times she said absolutely nothing. . . . Thinking back on it all, it must have been the most difficult part of mothering she ever had to do: knowing the outcome, yet feeling she had no right to keep me from charting my own path. I thank her for all her virtues, but mostly for never once having said, "I told you so."

ERMA BOMBECK

Where there is great love,
there are always miracles!

WILLA CATHER

———————◆———————

The modern challenge to motherhood is

the eternal challenge—that of being a godly woman.

The very phrase sounds strange in our ears. We never hear it now.

We hear about every other type of women: beautiful women,

smart women, sophisticated women, career women,

talented women, divorced women. But so seldom do we hear of

a godly woman—or of a godly man either, for that matter.

I believe women come nearer to fulfilling their

God-given function in the home than anywhere else.

PETER MARSHALL

Before you were conceived
I wanted you
Before you were born
I loved you
Before you were here an hour
I would die for you
This is the miracle of life.

MAUREEN HAWKINS

A family with an old person
has a living treasure of gold.

CHINESE PROVERB

What children need most

are the essentials that

grandparents provide in abundance.

They give unconditional love, kindness,

patience, humor, comfort, lessons in life.

And, most importantly,

cookies.

RUDOLPH GUILIANI

She who can paint a masterpiece or write a book that will influence millions deserves the plaudits and admiration of mankind. But she who would willingly and anxiously rear successfully a family of beautiful healthy sons and daughters whose lives reflect the teachings of the gospel, deserves the highest honors that man can give, and the choicest blessings of God. In fact, in her high duty and service to humanity, endowing with mortality eternal spirits, she is a co-partner with the Great Creator Himself.

DAVID O. McKAY

Behold, as the clay is in the potter's hand,
so are ye in mine hand, O house of Israel.

JEREMIAH 18:6

———————— ◆ ————————

Some mothers seem to have the capacity and energy to make their children's clothes, bake, give piano lessons, go to Relief Society, teach Sunday School, attend parent-teacher association meetings, and so on. Other mothers look upon such women as models and feel inadequate, depressed, and think they are failures when they make comparisons. . . . Sisters, do not allow yourselves to be made to feel inadequate or frustrated because you cannot do everything others seem to be accomplishing. Rather, each should assess her own situation, her own energy, and her own talents, and then choose the best way to mold her family into a team, a unit that works together and supports each other. Only you and your Father in Heaven know your needs, strengths, and desires. Around this knowledge your personal course must be charted and your choices made.

MARVIN J. ASHTON

 mother's heart
is the child's schoolroom.

HENRY WARD BEECHER

MOTHER'S LOVE

A mother's love is like an island
In life's ocean vast and wide,
A peaceful, quiet shelter
From the restless, rising tide. . . .

A mother's love is like a beacon
Burning bright with Faith and Prayer
And through the changing scenes of life
We can find a haven there. . . .

For a mother's love is fashioned
After God's enduring love,
It is endless and unfailing
Like the love of Him above.

For God knew in His great wisdom
That he couldn't be everywhere,
So he put His little Children
In a loving mother's care.

HELEN STEINER RICE

Living by basic good-mothering guidelines enables a mom to blend the responsibilities of parenthood with its joys; to know when to stand her ground and when to be flexible; and to absorb the lessons of the parenting gurus while also trusting her inner voice when it reasons that another cookie isn't worth fighting over, or that her child won't suffer irreparable trauma if, once in awhile, Mom puts her own needs first.

Sue Woodman

God could not be everywhere
and therefore he made mothers.

JEWISH PROVERB

In the Heavens above, the angels,

whispering to one another, can find,

among their burning terms of love,

none so devotional as that of 'Mother.'

EDGAR ALLAN POE

Motherhood is the greatest potential influence either for good or ill in human life. The mother's image is the first that stamps itself on the unwritten page of the young child's mind. It is her caress that first awakens a sense of security; her kiss, the first realization of affection; her sympathy and tenderness, the first assurance that there is love in the world.

David O. McKay

How thankful I am, how thankful we all must be,
for the women in our lives. God bless them.
May His great love distill upon them and crown them
with luster and beauty, grace and faith.

GORDON B. HINCKLEY

A mother is a woman
who shows you the light
when you just see the dark.

GRIMALDOS ROBIN

My mother is my root,
my foundation.
She planted the seed
that I base my life on,
and that is the belief
that the ability to achieve
starts in your mind.

MICHAEL JORDAN

If I had my child
to raise again,

I'd build self-esteem first,
    and the house later.

I'd finger-paint more,
    and point the finger less.

I would do less correcting,
    and more connecting.

I'd take my eyes off my watch,
    and watch with my eyes.

I'd take more hikes
    and fly more kites.

I'd stop playing serious,
    and seriously play.

I would run through more fields
    and gaze at more stars.

I'd do more hugging
    and less tugging.

DIANE LOOMANS

others have a sacred role. They are partners with God, as well as with their own husbands, first in giving birth to the Lord's spirit children and then in rearing those children so they will serve the Lord and keep his commandments. . . . Motherhood is a holy calling, a sacred dedication for carrying out the Lord's work, a consecration and devotion to the rearing and fostering, the nurturing of body, mind, and spirit of those who kept their first estate and who came to this earth for their second estate to learn and be tested.

SPENCER W. KIMBALL

I remember my mother's prayers and they have always followed me. They have clung to me all my life.

ABRAHAM LINCOLN

Blessed is the Mother . . .

Who can hold onto her children while letting them go;

Who puts a tranquil home ahead of an immaculate house;

Who knows a kind act will be remembered

longer than an easy word;

Who really believes that prayer changes things;

Whose faith in the future sweetens the present;

Whose Bible never needs dusting; and

Whose sense of humor is alive and well.

ANONYMOUS

And say to mothers
what a holy charge
Is theirs—with what a
kingly power their love
Might rule the fountains
of the new-born mind.

LYDIA HUNTLEY SIGOURNEY

aking the decision to have a child is momentous. It is to decide forever to have your heart go walking around outside your body.

ELIZABETH STONE

Don't get so involved in
the duties of your life
and your children
that you forget the pleasure.
Remember why you had children.

LOIS WYSE

Let France have good mothers,
and she will have good sons.

NAPOLEON BONAPARTE

———————

A mother is not a
person to lean on,
but a person to make leaning
unnecessary.

DOROTHY CANFIELD FISHER

Being a king, emperor, or president is mighty small potatoes compared to being a mother. Commanding an army is little more than sweeping a street compared with training a boy or girl. The mother of Moses did more for the world than all the kings that Egypt ever had. Oh, you wait until you reach the mountains of eternity, then read the mothers' names in God's Hall of Fame.

BILLY SUNDAY

The formative period for building character for eternity is in the nursery. The mother is queen of that realm and sways a scepter more potent than that of kings or priests.

ANONYMOUS

Who ran to help me
when I fell,
And would some
pretty story tell,
Or kiss the place
to make it well,
My mother.

ANN TAYLOR (MRS. GILBERT)

If you bungle raising your children,
I don't think whatever else you do well matters very much.

JACQUELINE KENNEDY ONASSIS

———— ◆ ————

I think every working mom goes through

the times when you feel that if you weren't working

perhaps you'd be giving them a little more.

I've always believed the quality of the time

is so much more important than the quantity.

JACKIE ZEMAN

It's a strange thing, but somehow we expect more of girls than of boys. It is the sisters and wives and mothers, you know, Caddie, who keep the world sweet and beautiful. What a rough world it would be if there were only men and boys in it, doing things in their rough way! A woman's task is to teach them gentleness and courtesy and love and kindness. It's a big task, too, Caddie—harder than cutting trees or building mills or damming rivers. It takes nerve and courage and patience, but good women have those things. They have them just as much as the men who build bridges and carve roads through the wilderness. A woman's work is something fine and noble to grow up to, and it is just as important as a man's.

EXCERPT FROM *CADDIE WOODLAWN*, BY CAROL RYRIE BRINK

Maybe I've been put on earth
to be an ordinary person.
Not to do anything great,
but to do something small
that involves great love.

ANONYMOUS MOTHER